THE HESYCHAST

Gregory of Sinai,
Archbishop of Constantinople

Translated by: D.P. Curtin

Dalcassian Publishing Company
PHILADELPHIA, PA

THE HESYCHAST

Copyright @ 2015 Dalcassian Publishing Company

All rights reserved. No part of this publication may be reproduced, distributed, or transmitted in any form or by any means, including photocopying, recording, or other electronic or mechanical methods, without the prior written permission of the publisher, except in the case of brief quotations embodied in critical reviews and certain other non-commercial uses permitted by copyright law. For permission request, write to Dalcassian Publishing Company at dalcassianpublishing at gmail.com

ISBN: 979-8-8690-2563-0 (Paperback)

Library of Congress Control Number:
Author: Curtin, D.P. (1985-)

Printed by Ingram Content Group, 1 Ingram Blvd, La Vergne, Tennessee

First printing edition 2015.

THE HESYCHAST

THE HESYCHAST MUST SIT IN PRAYER WITHOUT BEING IN A HURRY TO GET UP

Remain as long as possible sitting on the bench in the laborious position I mentioned; to relax, lie down on the mat, but for a short time and infrequently. Remain seated with great patience for the sake of Him who said: "persevere in prayer"; do not be in a hurry to get up due to intolerance of that painful ordeal required by the internal invocation of the mind and by prolonged immobility. The Prophet reminds us: "Pains attack me like those of a woman in childbirth".

Folded in on yourself, collect the thought in your heart, make sure that it is open and call the Lord Jesus for help. Your shoulders will be tired, and your head will be very sore, you persevere laboriously and lovingly seeking the Lord in your heart. The Kingdom of God suffers violence and the violent steal it. The Lord openly showed great love in these and these travails. Patience and perseverance are always the result of physical and mental hardships.

HOW TO PRAYER

The Fathers suggest reciting the entire invocation: "Lord Jesus Christ Son of God, have mercy on me" and this is easier. Do not pass frequently from one form to another giving in to indolence but do it only to keep your prayer uninterrupted. Furthermore, some teach to recite the invocation orally, others to repeat it with the mind. I recommend both to you, to overcome the tiredness that sometimes takes over the mind, other times takes over the lips. Therefore, one can pray in two ways: with the mind and with the lips, the important thing is that the oral invocation is made with peace and without agitation; the broken voice could suffocate the feeling and attention of the mind. This is necessary until the mind, trained by exercise, progresses and receives the strength of the Spirit for perfect and ardent prayer. Then he will no longer need the word, he will be incapable of it, content only to carry out his work totally and exclusively in thought.

HOW TO DISCIPLINE YOUR SPIRIT

Know that no one can discipline his thoughts by himself unless he is under the dominion of the Spirit. Thought is unruly, not that it is restless by nature, but negligence has radically marked it with a disposition to wander. For the transgression of the commandments of the One who generated us, he separated us from God, causing us to lose in the sensible world the clear perception of Him and the union with Him. Since then the wandering thought, far from God, has been dragged prisoner everywhere, and he has no other possibility of peace other than by submitting to God, remaining close to him and united joyfully, praying with assiduous perseverance and confessing his sins every day to Him who is ready to give his forgiveness to those who ask for it in humble condolence and they tirelessly invoke his holy Name.

Retention of the breath by pursing the lips disciplines the thought, but for a short time, because it begins to dissipate again. When the energy of prayer intervenes, it takes the reins of command and keeps it close to itself, freeing it from chains and restoring joy. It can happen that while the thought is fixed in prayer and still in the heart, the imagination begins to wander and become interested in other things. It is not subject to anyone, except those who, having reached perfection in the Holy Spirit, remain immobile in Christ Jesus.

ON HOW TO BANISH THOUGHTS

No beginner is able to banish a thought unless God does it first. Only the strong are capable of fighting and conquering thoughts. And even these cannot do it by themselves, but with God's help they move into battle against thoughts and take up his weapons. When thoughts come, invoke the Lord Jesus often and patiently, and you will see them flee; they cannot bear the fire of the heart lit by prayer, and they run away as if they were burned by a flame.

John Climacus warns us to flog our enemies by repeating the name of Jesus; our God is the devouring fire of evil. And the Lord is ready to help us, and quick to defend anyone who ardently implores him day or night. Those who have not yet achieved the discipline of prayer can defeat thoughts with another tactic, imitating Moses. If he keeps his eyes and arms turned towards the sky, God will drive away his thoughts. Then sit down again and patiently resume the course of your prayer. This method is good for those who have not yet achieved the energy of prayer.

Even those who possess the energy of prayer, when bodily passions, sloth and sensuality, strong and violent passions, begin to agitate them, will often have to get up and open their arms begging for help. Do not do this often to avoid illusion, and after a short time sit down again, otherwise the enemy may deceive your mind with fantasies that pretend to be the image of the truth. Only those who possess a pure and perfect mind can have their thoughts immune from evil, wherever they turn, whether above or below, or in the heart.

ON THE RECITATION OF THE PSALMS

Some maintain that the psalms should be said rarely, others frequently, still others that they should never be said.

I warn you to prefer the recitation of the psalms from time to time, so as not to fall into restlessness, and not to completely abandon psalmody, to avoid laxity and negligence, follow the example of those who rarely recite the psalms. Moderation is the best measure for both the learned and the learned. Frequent chanting is good for those immersed in active life, they ignore mental activity and lead a life immersed in troubles. Those who practice silence enjoy praying to God in their hearts and achieving mastery over their thoughts.

When, sitting in your cell, you feel that prayer is working in your heart, do not interrupt it to go and recite the psalms, unless it, with divine approval, abandons you first. If you did, you would abandon God who is speaking to you within to speak to him from outside and you would move from the heights to the plain. You would also disturb your mind away from calm thinking. Hesychia, as its name suggests, acts, but in peace and quiet. Our God is peace, beyond all confusion and turmoil.

Those who ignore prayer should engage in the frequent recitation of the psalms and remain in the multiplicity of commitments and should not stop until, after a continuous experience of toil, they have reached contemplation and discovered the spiritual prayer that was active within them.

The work of the hesychast is different, the work of the cenobite is different, anyone who remains faithful to their vocation will achieve salvation... Those who practice prayer based on hearsay or through readings done without a guide are lost. Whoever has tasted grace should recite the psalms with discretion, this is the teaching of the Fathers, and should attend to the practice of prayer. In moments of apathy recite psalms and read the sentences of the Fathers. The ship does not need oars when the wind keeps the sails full; when the wind blows enough it is easy to cross the salty sea of passions; but when there is calm it is kept in motion by oars or a tug.

Some object that the Holy Fathers and certain moderns practiced night vigils and uninterrupted psalmody, we respond to them with the Scriptures, that not everything is perfect in us, that enthusiasm and physical strength have their limits and that what It appears small to adults but may not actually be so, nor is what appears large to children necessarily perfect.

From the perfect everything is done with ease. For this reason, not all were ever active nor will they be active; no one follows the same path or follows the same discipline to the end. Many have passed from the active life to the contemplative one; ceasing all activity they celebrated their perpetual spiritual Sabbath and rejoiced in the Lord alone, nourished by divine food; because of the superabundant grace they were incapable of chanting and thinking of anything else. They have known contemplative amazement, even if for a short time, they have attended, partially, the supreme of desires. Others, however, followed the active path to the end, and obtained salvation by dying in the hope of receiving the future reward. Others received the testimony of salvation at the point of death, which manifested itself in a sweet aroma after death. These are those who have preserved the grace of baptism intact, but, due to the slavery and ignorance of their minds, were unable to participate while alive in the mysterious communion of grace. Others successfully practiced psalmody and prayer, rich in an always active grace and free from any hindrance. Others, although they were simple people, kept silent until the end, enjoying only the prayer which perfectly united them to God.

The perfect, as we have said, can do everything in their strength which is Jesus Christ to whom be glory forever and ever. Amen.

ON THE USE OF FOOD

What can I say about the belly which is the king of passions? If you manage to kill or destroy at least half of it, try to hold on to your conquest. It is a coterie of devils and the receptacle of passions; for him we fall, for him we get up when we manage to dominate him...

According to the teachings of the Fathers, nutrition differs greatly: some need little food, others are satisfied with enough to keep them strong, and are satisfied when the food supports their strength and conforms to their habits.

The hesychast must be economical in everything, nor must he indulge in excessive meals. When the stomach is heavy the mind remains clouded, and prayer cannot be practiced with clarity and consistency. Under the influence of the fumes of too much food, one becomes drowsy, and wishes to lie down to sleep; from this state derive the innumerable reveries that rush into the mind during sleep.

Whoever wants to reach salvation, and for the love of the Lord, does violence to lead a life of silence, must be content, in my opinion, with a pound of bread, three or four glasses of wine and water a day, and some other foods that he may have available. You don't eat your fill; by following this diet, i.e. by consuming every kind of food with moderation, on the one hand he will avoid vanity, on the other he will not show contempt for the gifts of God which are always good and he will be grateful to God for everything. Such is the behavior of the wise. Those who are of weak faith will find it advantageous to abstain from certain foods; the Apostle advises such men to feed on herbs, not believing that God is their only support.

Nutrition has three modes of behavior: abstinence, sufficiency, abundance. Abstinence means leaving the table feeling a little hungry; sufficiency means neither remaining hungry nor being overwhelmed by food. Eating beyond satiety opens the door to the madness of the belly, through which lust passes.

THE HESYCHAST

Be firm in this wisdom, choose what is best for you, taking into account your needs without ever going beyond the limits. The perfect man, according to the Apostle, must, "whether he is full or hungry, do all things for the love of Christ who makes him strong".

ON THE DETOUR

I want to tell you carefully about the deviation so that you can guard against it so that, due to ignorance, you do not suffer serious damage and lose your soul. The human will is easily inclined to orient itself towards the opposing party; in particular, those who lack experience are more exposed to the enemy. Demons love to lay the snares of thoughts and pernicious fantasies around beginners and extravagant people, and prepare traps to make them fall, their inner citadel being in the hands of barbarians. It is not surprising if someone has erred, or lost his intellect, having accepted deviation, following things contrary to the truth, and, due to lack of experience or ignorance, has seen or said unlikely things. It can happen that someone speaking ignorantly affirms one thing for another, and not knowing how to express himself correctly, disturbs his listeners and exposes himself and the hesychasts to derision and ridicule. Nothing strange that a beginner can get lost even after much effort: it has happened in the past and present to many who seek God.

The invocation of God, mental prayer is the highest work that man can perform, it is the summit of all virtues such as the love of God.

Anyone who recklessly undertakes the path that leads to God, to pure divine worship, to the possession of God within himself, is easy prey to demons if God abandons him. Seeking, with insolence and presumption, what does not correspond to his development, he strives to reach it ahead of time. The merciful God, seeing how hasty we are in wanting things that are beyond our possibilities, often does not leave us alone in temptation, because by noting our presumption he leads us back to the right actions, before we become the object of derision and ridicule to others. demons, of laughter and contempt on the part of men.

THE HESYCHAST

If you are practicing silence seriously, desiring union with God, do not allow an external sensitive or mental object, external or internal, even the image of Christ, or the form of an angel or a saint, or imaginary light, presents itself to your mind, do not accept it. The mind has a natural power to fantasize and easily builds fantastic images of what it desires if you are not vigilant and thus end up damaging yourself.

The memory of good or evil things is imprinted on the mind and leads it to fantasize. To whomever happens, instead of becoming a hesychast, he becomes a dreamer. For this reason, be careful not to immediately give faith and assent, even when it is a good thing, before having questioned an expert and investigated thoroughly, to avoid any possible risk. As a general rule, be wary of these images, keep your mind clear of colors, images and shapes.

If you work to achieve pure silent prayer, proceed with peace, but with great trepidation and compunction under the guidance of experienced masters. Continuously shed tears for your sins, with bitter compunction and fear of future punishments, and fear of being separated in this world and the other, from God.

The infallible prayer sent by God, as a foretaste of victory, has turned into harm for many. The Lord wants to test our free will to see which way it leans. Anyone who sees something in his thoughts in the senses or in his thoughts, and even admitting that it comes from God, adheres to it without first questioning the experts, will easily fall into error by being too willing and inclined to accept it.

It is good for the beginner to commit himself to the work of the heart, it does not deceive, and he does not accept anything before having triumphed over the passions. God is not displeased with those who strictly monitor themselves and refuse to accept what comes from Him without first questioning and investigating. Indeed, God praises his wisdom even if he has offended him in something.

The questions should not be addressed to the first person you meet, but to the one who has the divine gift of directing others, whose life is bright and who, despite being poor, enriches many. Many improvised in this task have harmed numerous naive people, for which they will account after their death. Not everyone has the ability to guide others: those who have received this mandate with the gift of divine discernment have it, as the apostle writes of that discernment of spirits, I mean, which separates good from evil with the sword of the word . Everyone can be endowed with both practical and scientific discriminative abilities, not everyone has the discernment of spirits.

Prayer is ardent when it is accompanied by the invocation of Jesus. He brings fire to the region of the heart. Its flame burns the passions like chaff, and fills the heart with joy and peace; it descends into us neither from the right, nor from the left nor from above, it erupts in the heart as a source from the life-giving Spirit.

This is the prayer you must desire to find and reach in your heart; keeps the mind free from daydreams and free from thoughts and reasoning. And don't be fearful. He who says: "Trust, it is I, do not be afraid, is truly within us; We seek Him and He always protects us." When we call upon the Lord we must neither be afraid nor sigh.

If anyone has gone astray and lost his mind, it was, believe me, because he followed his own whim and pride.

Whoever seeks God in submission, and humbly questions those who are more expert, will not have to fear any damage for the grace of Christ who wants to save all men. Those who practice silent prayer always follow this royal path. Excess in any direction produces presumption which is followed by confusion. Control the rhythm of your thoughts, pursing your lips a little during prayer, don't worry about the rhythm of your nostrils like fools do, so as not to succumb to pride.

THE HESYCHAST

There are three qualities of silent prayer: austerity, silence, non-consideration of oneself, that is, humility; these must be practiced faithfully; we must continually check whether they are our home, because by forgetting them we do not set out outside them. One supports and safeguards the other, prayer is born from them and grows perfectly.

THE CONTEMPLATIVE LIFE AND THE TWO WAYS OR PRAYER

There are two ways of union with God, more precisely there are two entrances for mental prayer that the spirit awakens in the heart.

One occurs when the mind "closely clinging to the Lord" quickly enters the abode of prayer; the other when the prayerful activity takes place gradually and through a joyful fire exercises the mind and keeps it firm with the unitive invocation of the Lord Jesus. The Spirit works in each according to his good pleasure, it is therefore possible that one form of union precedes the other in the various persons, in the way I have said above. Other times, when the passions are weakened by the constant invocation of Jesus Christ, the event accompanied by a divine fervor manifests itself in the heart. "God is a fire that consumes" passions. In other cases the spirit attracts the mind to itself, welding it into the heart and preventing the usual wandering of thoughts.

ON THE EXERCISE OF PRAYER

At dawn sow the seed, the prayer, in the evening your hand does not remain idle, says Solomon; this is so that the prayer is not interrupted and risks losing the hour of answering, "you don't know which of the two sowings will give you fruit".

Early in the morning, sit on a stool a foot high; direct the thought from the dominion of the mind to the heart and force it to remain there. Hunched laboriously, while your chest, shoulders and neck will hurt, cry out with perseverance and with thought and soul: "Lord Jesus Christ, have mercy on me". Subsequently, whether due to the forced position, or the boredom caused by the prolonged pause on the same formula, bring your thoughts to the other form of the invocation and repeat: "Son of God, have mercy on me!". Repeat this formula numerous times, avoid, out of indolence, changing it too often, plants transplanted frequently do not take root.

Control the breathing of the lungs, so as not to breathe in the usual way. Since the breath of uncontrolled breaths that rises from the heart darkens the mind and agitates the soul, dissipates it, abandons it to distraction, or makes all sorts of images pass before it, insensitively directing it towards what is not good. Do not be troubled if you see the impurity of evil spirits arise and take shape in your thoughts; as well as not paying attention to the good thoughts that may come to you. Keep your mind firm in your heart, dominate your breathing, and repeat the invocation to the Lord Jesus without tiring; soon you will burn and dominate these thoughts, flogging them invisibly with the divine Name. John Climacus says: "With the name of Jesus he scourges his enemies. There is no stronger weapon, neither in heaven nor on earth".

ON CONTROLLED BREATHING

Isaiah the hermit and with him many others, regarding the control of breathing says: "Dominate the tireless thought, that is, the mind agitated and distracted by the power of the enemy who, due to negligence, has returned, even after Baptism, to the lazy soul, followed by numerous evil spirits", in accordance with what the Lord said: "the last condition of man is worse than the first". Another says: "Let the monk have the invocation of God instead of breathing." Another: "The love of God must precede breathing." Simon the New Theologian: "Compress the rhythm of breathing so as not to breathe in the usual way." John Climacus warns: "Let the memory of Jesus be united to your breathing, you will learn the strength of silence". And the Apostle Paul states: "Not I, but Christ lives in me" working in him by breathing divine life into him. And the Lord says: "the Spirit blows where he wants", taking the image of the wind that blows. When we were purified in baptism, we received the inheritance of the Spirit and the seeds of the inner word.

Having neglected the commandments, guardians of grace, we have again fallen into passions, and instead of breathing the Holy Spirit, we have filled ourselves with the breath of evil spirits. From them originate yawning and stretching of the limbs, according to the Fathers. Whoever has welcomed the Spirit and allowed himself to be purified by Him is also warmed by Him and breathes divine life, speaks it, thinks it, and lives it, in accordance with the words of the Lord. "It is not you who speaks but the Spirit of the Father who speaks in you". In the same way, those who are inhabited by a spirit opposed to the Lord speak and act in a manner contrary to the Lord.

CONTEMPLATION AND PRAYER

1. We should speak like the Great Doctor, St. Paul, without needing the Scriptures or the teachings of the other Fathers, or the illustrious Longinus, aware of being directly "taught by God", in order to learn and know the important things in Him and through Him. In fact, we were called to guard the Tablets of the Law of the Spirit engraved in our hearts, to converse with Jesus through pure prayer, without intermediaries as if we were Cherubim.

2. I will begin by saying with the help of God who gives the word to those who announce these goods, how one can find Christ received in the baptism of the Spirit (don't you know that the Spirit dwells in your heart?); so how can we move forward; finally, the ways of preserving what has been found. Beginners have action as their starting point; those who are along the path attain enlightenment; those who have reached the end find purification and resurrection of the soul.

3. There are two ways to find the energy of the Spirit which was sacramentally given to us in Baptism:

a - the practice, at the cost of prolonged efforts, of the commandments: allows the revelation of this gift. Saint Mark tells us: "to the extent that we practice the commandments it makes its light shine in us".

b - through submission, achieved with the methodical and constant invocation of the Lord Jesus, that is, with the memory of God. The longer the path of the first way, the quicker that of the second, as long as one has learned to dig the earth with vigor and perseverance to discover gold. Wanting to discover and know the truth without error, let us try to reach the energy of the heart by placing ourselves beyond forms and figures, freeing the imagination from any form or impression of things called holy, nor stopping to contemplate any light. Let us try to keep active in our hearts the energy of prayer which gives warmth and joy to the mind, and which lights up in the soul an unspeakable love towards God and towards men. No small humility and contrition will arise from prayer; prayer being, even for beginners, the tireless action of the Spirit that begins in the heart as a joyful fire and ends in a light that spreads a sweet odor.

4. The signs of this beginning for those who truly commit themselves can be: a light of dawn; a joy combined with trepidation; or pure joy, or joy mixed with fear, or fear interwoven with joy; and also tears and anguish. The soul rejoices in the presence and mercy of God, trembles thinking of the divine visitation and its innumerable sins. In others the encounter produces an unspeakable contrition and an inexpressible torment of the soul, almost the pain of a woman in labor mentioned in Scripture. The living and active word of God, who is Jesus Christ, goes so far as to divide the soul from the body, the joints from the marrow, to eliminate from the soul and the body what still contains passion. Others, however, experience a sort of unspeakable love and peace towards all beings; others, however, feel an exultation and a jubilation, called by the Fathers: movement of the living heart, energy of the spirit. This phenomenon is also called the impulse and inexpressible sigh of the Spirit who intercedes for us before God. Isaiah names it the "wave of God's justice"; and the great Ephrem calls it 'wound'; the Lord: Source of water that flows for eternal life, water is the spirit that flows and gurgles powerfully in the heart.

The beginnings of grace in prayer are manifested differently, according to the Apostle, the Spirit divides his gifts in accordance with his will. Elijah Tesbite offers us an example. In some the spirit of fear passes by splitting mountains, crumbling rocks, hardening hearts, in such a way that to the flesh it seems pierced by nails and left for dead. In others, a movement is produced, an exultation, called by the Fathers a leap, immaterial but internally substantial: substantial because that which has no essence or substance cannot exist. In others, chiefly in those who are advanced in prayer, God produces a bright breeze, light and pleasant, while Christ takes up residence in the heart and mysteriously appears in the Spirit. This is why on Mount Horeb God said to Elijah: The Lord is not in the first or second state, in the personal actions of beginners, but in the light aura of light, indicating perfect prayer.

5. It must be kept in mind that exultation and jubilation can be of two types, one is tranquil and is the impulse, the groan, the intimate action of the Spirit; and an intense one, the startle, the momentum, the powerful flight of the living heart in the divine sky. The soul freed from passions receives wings from the divine Spirit that lead it to love.

8. Two distinct energies operate in the heart of every beginner: one that comes from grace, the other that comes from error. Mark the great hermit talks about it like this: "There is a spiritual energy and a satanic energy unknown to beginners." And furthermore: threefold is the flame that burns in man's energies, one is lit by grace, the second is brought by error and sin, the third comes from the superabundance of blood. Thalassios the African calls the latter: temperament, and this can be tamed and pacified with balanced abstinence.

9. The energy of grace is a fiery force of the Spirit that moves with joy and delight in the heart; it consolidates, warms and purifies the soul, calms irritated thoughts, and for a while extinguishes the impulses of the flesh. These are the signs of his presence and the fruits that reveal the truth: tears, the condolence of sins, humility, the dominion of physical strength, silence, patience, love of solitude, all this fills the soul of a sense of undoubted fullness.

10. The activity of sin is the fever of sin which inflames the soul with voluptuousness, and by vigorously adhering to carnal lusts awakens the movements of the body. San Diadoco tells us that it is completely vulgar and disorderly. It brings with it unreasonable joy, vanity, disturbance, base pleasure and, as it is right to say, being devoid of substance, it acts preferably in those temperaments that delight in lukewarmness. Procuring inflamed matter, it collaborates with passions and with the insatiable belly. There it enters into relationship with the carnal complexion, inflaming it, it agitates the soul and overheats it, inviting it to itself, so that man, getting used to the pleasures of passion, slowly distances himself from grace.

The Scriptorium Project is the work of a small group of lay people of various apostolic churches who are interested in the preservation, transmission, and translation of the works of the early and medieval church. Our efforts are to make the works of the church fathers accessible to anyone who might have an interest in Christian antiquities and the theological, philosophical, and moral writings that have become the bedrock of Western Civilization.

To-date, our releases have pulled from the Greek, Syriac, Georgian, Latin, Celtic, Ethiopian, and Coptic traditions of Christianity, and have been pulled from sundry local traditions and languages.

Other Selections from the Byzantine Church Series:

Treatise on Sobriety by Nicephorus the Solitary (Apr. 2007)
Sermons by Nestorius of Constantinople (May 2009)
Theophrastus by Aeneas of Gaza (Apr. 2011)
Treatise on Prayer by St. Evargius of Ponticus (May 2011)
The Lausiac History by St. Palladius of Galatia (Mar. 2013)
Letter on the Fall of Constantinople by Isidore of Kiev (Oct. 2013)
The Hesychast by Gregory of Sinai (June 2015)
Selected Laws by Justinian I, Emperor of Rome (July 2018)
Exhortation to Monks Ordained in India by St. John of Karpathos (March 2021)
Fragments of 'Chronicle' by Hippolytus of Thebes (May 2023)
The Life of the Blessed Theotokos by Epiphanius Monachus (July 2023)
Letters of Nestorius by Nestorius of Constantinople (Sept. 2023)

THE HESYCHAST

www.ingramcontent.com/pod-product-compliance
Lightning Source LLC
LaVergne TN
LVHW061044070526
838201LV00073B/5172